Topic 1
Religious experience

G000155236

Experiences of God

This is an important and challenging area of philosophy of religion as it involves the most personal of the kind of evidence philosophers investigate. Here we are exploring what people say about their alleged experiences of God. One of the most famous remarks which highlights the issues in this part of the specification was from Thomas Hobbes, who said that when a man says that God spoke to him in a dream he is actually saying no more than he dreamed that God spoke to him.

A vitamin B deficiency is one of the things which cause alcoholics to have delirium tremens, which leads to hallucinations. Some might say this is no different from a holy man fasting, having the same deficiency, and seeing God. This is why Russell said that some people drink too much and see snakes while others fast too much and see God.

Studies of this phenomenon

A significant study of this phenomenon was done by William James and delivered as *The Varieties of Religious Experience* in his Gifford lectures in Edinburgh in 1901–02. The published book is still considered a seminal work in this area. In it he laid out the now famous characteristics of a mystical experience. The key words are passivity, ineffability, noetic and transient. It is important to keep in mind that he is not saying that the existence of these in an experience means that God exists but that they are commonly found in descriptions from those who claim to have had a religious experience.

The range of religious experiences is one of the things which make this area of study difficult. Most are reported as 'seeing' or 'auditory' experiences. Swinburne also divides these experiences into public and private. The strange events at Medjugorje for example would be considered a public experience as would descriptions of the sun standing still and the moon stopping in the Old Testament book of Joshua 10:13, whereas the experiences described by St Teresa of Avila are clearly very private events and as such may be valid only to the person having the experience.

In evaluating these alleged experiences, you may find it useful to explore arguments around the area of what can be empirically verified. So while many would say that the alleged events at Fatima and Medjugorje or in the lives of individual believers cannot be empirically verified there is often evidence of profound changes in the way the people involved behave after the experience. So, for example, St Paul after his famous blinding and auditory experience on the road to Damascus changed from a persecutor of Christians to, arguably, the greatest Christian evangelist in history.

Corporate religious experiences

It is important to keep in mind that even corporate religious experiences are only valid for the individual experience within a group. Studies of group behaviour indicate that some within the event will claim to have the same experience as others when in fact they are simply behaving like the group but having no genuine experience themselves.

3

Here you may assess the truth or otherwise of Freud's claim that religious experience, whether private or corporate, is no more than wish fulfilment. He believed that religion is a 'universal obsessional neurosis' and that therefore these events are no more than the mind creating illusions to help the psyche cope with a frightening and chaotic world.

Alternatively, you could evaluate the Marxist view that religious illusions help humanity cope with a world devoid of dignity and full of degrading and empty experiences. The direction your assessment goes is up to you: examiners will judge your justification of your conclusions.

1 What is meant by religious experiences?

....

....

....

....

2 What is the importance of William James' Gifford lectures?

....

....

....

....

3 What did William James mean by the following?

passivity..

....

....

....

ineffability..

....

....

....

noetic...

....

....

....

transient...

....

....

④ Explain, with examples, what Swinburne means by experiences which are:

private ....

....

....

....

public ....

....

....

....

⑤ Describe what happened to St Paul on his way to Damascus.

....

....

....

....

....

⑥ Fill in the following Old Testament quotation:

"'Sun stand still over Gibeon,

....

....

....

till the nation avenged itself on its enemies.'

⑦ Describe one religious experience had by a saint such as St Teresa of Avila.

....

....

....

....

....

....

⑧ Describe one alleged corporate religious experience.

....

....

....

....

....

....

9 Assess Freud's critique of religious experience.

....

....

....

....

....

10 How does Dr Susan Blackmore explain that near death experiences are not experiences of God?

....

....

....

....

....

11 How might a religious believer respond to this critique?

....

....

....

....

....

12 How would David Hume have assessed religious experiences?

....

....

....

....

....

13 Summarise the issues for and against religious experience.

....

....

....

....

....

Exam-style question

Plan your answer here then write the answer itself on a separate sheet of paper. Allow 40 minutes to write this essay. Use 2 minutes to plan and 2 minutes to reread your essay and correct mistakes.

'Corporate religious experiences prove the existence of God.' Discuss.   35 marks   45

© OCR 2009–13

Topic 2
Miracles

This topic may be viewed as a specific extension of Topic 1. Miracles are often seen as a form of religious experience but a form that raises even more questions for the believer. Why, for example, would Jesus obey his mother at a wedding feast and turn water into wine while doing nothing about foreigners oppressing his own people? The *Oxford English Dictionary* defines a miracle 'as an extraordinary event that is not explicable by natural or scientific laws and is therefore attributed to a divine agency'.

Hume's criticisms of miracles

One of the main critics of belief in miracles was David Hume. He listed four reasons to question the validity of alleged miracles, brought about by his belief that miracles are inductively improbable. These are:

1 It is impossible to judge whether or not those claiming these experiences are being deceived, deluded or are in fact lying.
2 Human beings love to be dazzled by mysterious and miraculous events which often lead them to form unreasonable beliefs which should not be trusted.
3 These stories about unexplainable events are most often found among 'primitive and barbarous people' who lack the sophistication to understand what is really happening.
4 All kinds of faiths make miraculous claims in support of their own belief system which cannot all be true at the same time so they cancel each other out.

These are a necessarily brief summary of Hume's' conclusions. A good place to start an exploration of Hume would be by using Swinburne's two principles:

- the Principle of Testimony where he proposes that people generally do tell the truth
- the Principle of Credulity which argues that in general people ought to be believed unless there is evidence of some sort of personal impairment which would raise questions about their reliability

Your understanding of these complex questions should be developed through a study of the views on miracles proposed by Holland and Hick.

Maurice Wiles and 'selected miracles'

Maurice Wiles was an Anglican minister who raised some of the most challenging questions about the existence of miracles by questioning the kind of God who would work selected miracles at all. His principal concern therefore was in exploring the moral and theological implications of miracles. In summary, a God who works miracles is both arbitrary and partial. Or to put this concept another way, why would God cure a single person at Lourdes but allow 18 million people to be killed in the Nazi holocaust? Parting the Red Sea was good for Moses and the Hebrews but not so good for Pharaoh and his people.

It was important to Wiles that Jesus seemed to have refused to demonstrate his divinity by working miracles. He therefore concluded that miracles could not occur as the God he believed in does not intervene in human events on an individual basis. Hence he argued that 'The primary usage for the idea of divine action should be in relation to the world as a whole rather than to particular occurrences within it.' The world as a whole then is a single act of God and he should not be looked for in endless little adjustments to creation.

1 **How would David Hume define a miracle?**

....

....

2 **Complete the following definition of miracles from Aquinas:**

'Two things may be considered in miracles. ....

....

....

but on account of some excellence they receive the name of wonder or prodigy, as

showing something from afar.'

3 **Recount the story Holland uses as an example to show that miracles may be no more than coincidences.**

....

....

....

....

....

....

4 **Explain the principle of induction used in Hume's writings.**

....

....

....

....

5 **Summarise the conclusion which Hume holds about miracles.**

....

....

....

....

....

6 For Hume, human error was an everyday event whereas miracles were not. List the four additional points this led Hume to make.

Point 1 ....
....
....

Point 2 ....
....
....

Point 3 ....
....
....

Point 4 ....
....

7 Explain John Hick's view on miracles.
....
....
....
....
....

8 Explain the implication for belief in miracles of Bultmann's demythologising of the New Testament.
....
....
....
....
....

9 Explain why Maurice Wiles believed that belief in miracles is damaging to faith.
....
....
....
....
....
....

10 What might scientists such as Peter Atkins and Richard Dawkins say about miracles?

....

....

....

....

....

....

....

11 Explain how Keith Ward has responded to Wiles' view on miracles.

....

....

....

....

....

....

....

....

12 Explain what Swinburne means when he says that the laws of nature are probabilistic.

....

....

....

....

....

....

....

....

13 Which description of miracles do you think is more likely and why? Coincidences, acts of God or simply illusions?

....

....

....

....

....

....

....

Exam-style question

Answer the following question on a separate sheet of paper. Allow 40 minutes to write this essay. Use 2 minutes to plan and 2 minutes to reread your essay and correct mistakes.

Evaluate the view that miracles are the least likely of events.　**35 marks** 45

Topic 3
Via negativa and analogy

The *via negativa*

Speaking about a being who, by definition, is ineffable, clearly has difficulties. In this and the next few topics we will explore attempts to overcome some of these problems. First, there is the *via negativa* or apophatic way (a Greek neologism which suggests the collapse of language in the face of the infinite). This proposes that, since we cannot say what God is, as our language is not capable of expressing accurate knowledge of God, we are left with saying what he is not. For example, if we describe God as 'timeless', we have no real conception of what that really means in relation to God. So those who follow the apophatic way are left describing God by saying, he is not temporal, he is not finite, he is not evil and so on.

One of the most famous proponents of this system of religious language was a sixth-century philosopher named Pseudo-Dionysius who distinguished between the cataphatic (*via positiva*) and the apophatic. This method of talking about God reappears throughout history. In the ninth century John Scotus translated much of the work of Pseudo-Dionysius and his influence can be seen in Scotus' own writings. Then the writings of the medieval philosopher Moses Maimonides, who had adopted the *via negativa*, influenced the philosophy of Thomas Aquinas and hence came into what he called a prelude to the Christian understanding of the nature of God.

Aquinas and analogy

Aquinas recognised the need for Christians to find a way of talking about God in a positive way while recognising the challenge of the *via negativa*. This led him to develop the 'Doctrine of Analogy'. To follow this you need to make sure you understand what he means by what he describes as three significant types of language — namely univocal, equivocal and analogical.

Here we will just look at the analogy of attribution and the analogy of proportion. By 'analogy of attribution' Aquinas meant that we might attribute a word like 'good' to God in much the same way as we apply the word to different things in ordinary language. Brian Davies, for example, uses the idea of both a baker and his bread as being good but clearly the word is not used in the same way for each. So for God to be called good may be similar as an attribution but not the same as a human being described as good. Aquinas points out that we may be good by resisting temptation but we would not apply this sense to God. Also God is the source of goodness for Christians and it is through the goodness of his creation that we learn what goodness means.

This leads naturally to the idea of proportion. A good laptop does all the things that a good laptop is expected to do; a good person does all the things a good person would be expected to do. When it comes to God, Aquinas says that he is perfectly good in the sense that he lives up to all that you would expect a divinity to do. Keep in mind that this is not moral goodness but a goodness that is unchangeable and eternal. This does have its problems, however, as we cannot really move from what I expect a good laptop to do while I am typing this to what it is to be a good God. Since his nature is so different from ours and we can never fully know what it is to be a good God then is the language itself in fact meaningless?

Ultimately, what we have here are some of the attempts to talk about God with a limited and finite language which attempts to express beliefs about a divinity of which we can have no empirical knowledge and which is by its very nature a mystery. Perhaps the best that can be said of the *via negativa* is that it stops the tendency among some believers to anthropomorphise God and that analogy allows us to say something about God albeit in a very limited way.

1 Write out your own definition of the apophatic way.

....

....

....

....

2 Describe the cataphatic way.

....

....

....

....

3 Describe the views on the *via negativa* of Pseudo-Dionysius.

....

....

....

....

....

....

....

4 Describe the beliefs of Moses Maimonides on religious language.

....

....

....

....

....

....

....

5 To what extent is it possible to talk about God without anthropomorphising him?

....

....

....

....

....

....

6 What does Aquinas mean by univocal language?

....

....

....

....

....

7 What does Aquinas mean by equivocal language?

8 What does Aquinas mean by analogical language?

9 In your own words and using your own examples describe the analogy of attribution.

10 In your own words and using your own examples describe the analogy of proportion.

11 The analogy of proportion raises questions in terms of understanding the scale of that proportion. Describe Baron von Hügel's attempt to clarify this point.

12 Explain what Ramsey meant when he said that words and titles applied to God function as 'models'.

....
....
....
....
....
....
....
....

13 What does Ramsey mean by the term 'qualifier'?

....
....
....
....
....
....
....

14 Why does Karl Barth argue that both analogy in general and Ramsey in particular are wrong in their approach to religious language?

....
....
....
....
....
....
....
....
....

15 Explain which of these attempts to talk about God you find most useful and why.

....
....
....
....
....
....
....
....
....
....

Exam-style question

Plan your answer here then write the answer itself on a separate sheet of paper. Allow 40 minutes to write this essay. Use 2 minutes to plan and 2 minutes to reread your essay and correct mistakes.

Evaluate the claim that analogy can be used to express the human understanding of God.

35 marks 45

© OCR 2009–13

Topic 4
Symbol and myth

Symbols and symbolic language

Another attempt to communicate knowledge about God is found through the use of symbols and symbolic language. It is important when exploring this area that you distinguish between the use of symbols, symbolic actions and symbolic language.

Paul Tillich uses two, suggesting that we teach and talk about God through such things as the crucifix and equally through describing God as a shepherd or a warrior. He describes God as the 'Ground of our Being'. By this he means that without God nothing will exist — he is the reason that there is something rather than nothing and, to paraphrase Aquinas, all else is straw compared with this knowledge. Descriptions of Jesus, for example, as Son of Man, Son of God, Messiah, Healer or Shepherd are to be taken as symbolic attempts to describe a mystery.

Tillich also says that symbols participate in that to which they point, though he is unclear as to exactly what he means by that concept. The meaning given to these symbols comes from the culture within which they originate and their importance is often dependent on that culture. So while flags are important all over the world not many countries use them as a pledge of allegiance. The importance of this symbol in the USA not only means it is used daily in schools but also means it can be burned as a symbol by those who hate, for example, the legacies of US policies in the Middle East.

The cultural significance of symbols means that over time some lose their meaning and others change their meaning. The Hindu symbol of a Swastika moved from being a symbol of peace to a very different meaning under the Nazis.

Tillich says if I say God is just or God is truth the terms are both 'affirmed and negated by the reality of God'. They are affirmed because we believe that God is both just and true but negated because human language is staggeringly inadequate when we attempt to speak of God.

Myth

Myth is a concept which seems to be notoriously hard for students to grasp. While myths are made up of stories and legends that sit in our minds as things which are untrue, religious myths claim to contain truths which are difficult to express in any other way. Creation myths, for example, are the most common type of this written form. Parts of the Genesis creation story can be found in the Babylonian myth known as *Enuma Elis*, though the aims of the two texts are different. The Babylonians wanted to raise their god, Marduk, above other gods in their region whereas the Hebrews wanted to explain the existence of the universe through the volition of their one God, Yahweh.

The key idea to keep in mind is that these myths attempt to express a truth to the people using them. In the Judaeo-Christian tradition, Genesis would not, by most, be thought of as literally true but to contain the truth of the universe's dependence on one God who both made and sustains our world. So these are more than just stories to entertain children, they are intended to communicate the values and beliefs of the communities from which they originated.

Those outside these communities may say the stories are meaningless but that does not reduce their importance to those who build their lives around the values found in their own myths. In this sense myths can be seen as being very like symbols in the specificity of their significance.

1 Give an example of a religious symbol and explain its importance to the community within which it originated.

....

....

....

....

2 Give an example of religious symbolic language and explain its importance to the community within which it originated.

....

....

....

....

3 Give an example of a non-religious myth and explain its importance to the community within which it originated.

....

....

....

....

4 Explain the distinction which Tillich makes between a sign and a symbol.

....

....

....

....

....

5 Explain the issue raised by John Hick about the difficulties in understanding what Tillich meant by a symbol participating in that to which it points.

....

....

....

....

6 Describe Randall's non-cognitivist analysis of religious language.

....

....

....

....

....

7 Explain the aims of the writers of the *Enuma Elis*.

....

....

....

....

....

8 Compare the Judaeo-Christian myth of creation with the *Enuma Elis*.

....

....

....

....

....

9 Describe Bultmann's views on demythologising the New Testament.

....

....

....

....

....

....

....

10 How do symbols and myths communicate values and truths?

....

....

....

....

....

....

....

Exam-style question

Answer the following question on a separate sheet of paper. Allow 40 minutes to write this essay. Use 2 minutes to plan and 2 minutes to reread your essay and correct mistakes.

Critically compare the use of myth with the use of analogy to express the human understanding of God.

`35 marks` `45`

© OCR 2009–13

Topic 5
The verification principle

The Vienna Circle

The main aim of the Vienna Circle, who introduced the verification principle to the world, was to demonstrate that religious language is meaningless. As well as reacting against idealist metaphysics, its members were influenced by the *Tractatus Logico Philosophicus* of Wittgenstein. Keep in mind though that Wittgenstein was never part of the Circle and was not its founder. The Circle was founded after conversations, in 1907, between Otto Neurath, Hans Hahn and Philip Frank. However, it was in 1922 when Maurice Schlick took over its leadership that it became a real force in philosophy.

Since members were mainly scientists they felt that it was not the place of philosophers to describe the world. If anyone wished to know something about the world they should ask a scientist. The job of philosophy was to analyse sentences to see whether or not they were meaningful or just nonsense. This led them to argue that there were only two kinds of meaningful propositions: those which are tautologies and those which are empirically verifiable.

A. J. Ayer and verifiability

So how do we check the verifiability of a statement? A. J. Ayer suggested that you need to distinguish between practical verifiability and verifiability in principle. If you are told that there is a building called the Shard in London then you can verify this through looking in London and through that having the empirical evidence. However, a statement such as there was once life on Mars is not verifiable at the moment but is in principle verifiable when technology has advanced sufficiently to make a full scientific study of Mars possible. A. J. Ayer further divided verifiable propositions into what he described as strong and weak verification. In *Language, Truth and Logic*, he wrote:

> A proposition is said to be verifiable, in the strong sense of the term, if and only if, its truth could be conclusively established in experience. But it is verifiable, in the weak sense, if it is possible for experience to render it probable.

It is clear then that when this principle is applied to a religious statement there is no way that it can be considered meaningful. To say that God exists is, for a verificationist, meaningless or nonsense. The same is true for the atheist who says that God does not exist; the statement is no less meaningless. When you explore this further you will find that Ayer had a preference for the weak version of this principle as he had issues with the reliability of the strong version.

Is the verification principle meaningless?

The initial weakness to this theory is that the verification principle itself is neither a tautology nor empirically verifiable. As its truth cannot be demonstrated by any process of observation, it fails its own rules and should therefore be considered meaningless. So anyone who wants to hold the verification principle as itself true is committing themselves to a form of foundationalism.

You should also question the implied assumption that one can in fact reduce sentences to two classes, that they are either verifiable by being open to scientific investigation, or else they are meaningless. Clearly it is not as self-evident as the logical positivists want us to believe that sentences can be split into these two classes.

1 a Otto Neurath was a ....

   b Hans Hahn was a ....

   c Philip Frank was a ....

   d Maurice Schlick was a ....

2 What are logical positivists?

....

....

....

....

....

3 Why were Frege, Russell and Whitehead significant to the Vienna Circle?

....

....

....

....

....

4 Explain, using an example, what is meant by a tautology.

....

....

....

....

....

....

5 What is meant by empirically verifiable?

....

....

6 In your own words explain what A. J. Ayer meant by strong verification.

....

....

....

....

7 In your own words explain what A.J. Ayer meant by weak verification.

....

....

....

....

....

8 Fill in the gaps in the following quotation:

It will be our contention that no proposition, other than a tautology, can possibly be more than a probable hypothesis. ....

.... For it leads to the conclusion that

it is impossible to make a significant statement of fact at all.

9 Explain what you think Ayer meant by the statement in question 8.

....

....

....

10 Research and explain what is meant by foundationalism.

....

....

....

....

11 Why might the logical positivists be considered as foundationalists?

....

....

....

....

12 What are protocol statements, as used by the logical positivists?

....

....

....

13 What issues are raised by this response to the self-refuting problem of the verification principle?

....

....

....

....

....

....

⑭ Explain eschatological verification using Hick's story of the Celestial City.

....

....

....

....

....

⑮ What is meant by the phrase 'eschatological verification is asymmetrical'?

....

....

....

....

⑯ Explain the critique of verification raised by Vincent Brümmer.

....

....

....

....

....

⑰ Explain the critique of verification put forward by D. Z. Phillips.

....

....

....

....

....

....

Exam-style question

Answer the following question on a separate sheet of paper. Allow 40 minutes to write this essay. Use 2 minutes to plan and 2 minutes to reread your essay and correct mistakes.

Critically assess the claim that religious language is meaningless.   `35 marks`   `45`

© OCR 2009–13

Topic 6
The falsification symposium

Popper and the falsification principle

Probably the most important challenge to logical positivism was put forward by Karl Popper. He based his opposition to the Vienna Circle against their assumption that what mattered was to be able to prove scientific propositions true. He rightly pointed out that if we based scientific investigations around proving a hypothesis to be true then we would make no progress at all. He therefore claimed that what we should be interested in is what would falsify our claims. Proving all or parts of scientific theories false and trying to improve on them is the process by which science moves forward. This led him to propose the falsification principle which, rather than being a criterion of meaning, was about the scientific status of a proposition.

The *University* debate

The best place to explore this area of the specification is to study the *University* debate between Flew, Mitchell and Hare. Flew starts with Wisdom's parable of two travellers who on finding a garden argue about whether or not a gardener exists. In essence this parable is about believers continually, as it were, moving the goal posts. Whenever someone says there is no evidence for your belief here or there they say something like: it is a mystery and we cannot have evidence. This is what led Flew to describe religious belief as dying the death of a thousand qualifications.

The challenge he made to the symposium was:

> Just what would have to happen not merely (morally and wrongly) to tempt but also (logically and rightly) to entitle us to say 'God does not love us' or even 'God does not exist'? I therefore put to the succeeding symposiasts the simple central questions, 'What would have to occur or to have occurred to constitute a disproof of the love of, or of the existence of God?'

Hare replied by introducing the idea of 'bliks' which he maintains we all have. They are beliefs which may be neither verifiable nor falsifiable. The example he uses is of a university student who believes that his lecturers are out to kill him and nothing anyone says will persuade him that he is wrong. Through this, Hare maintains that bliks have a profound effect on the lives of people. So when we make a religious statement it not only describes our view of the world around us but is life-changing even though it is by its nature unfalsifiable. Flew believes that Hare's view is vulnerable to the following criticism:

> Religious utterances may indeed express false or even bogus assertions: but I simply do not believe that they are not both intended and interpreted to be or at any rate to presuppose assertions, at least in the context of religious practice.

Basil Mitchell proposed a stronger challenge to Flew through his story of the partisan. He wanted to be able to hold that religious utterances could be genuinely factual while not necessarily being falsifiable. Through his parable of the partisan, Mitchell was trying to create a situation where some evidence pointed to one of the resistance leaders being a collaborator and other evidence pointed the other way. Mitchell did point out there is a point beyond which the partisan could not continue to hold his view. Another way of thinking of this parable is to consider all of Harry Potter's attempts to convince Dumbledore that Snape was still a Deatheater. In the stories the partisan and Dumbledore not only have faith in their people but consider that they have reason for their faith.

As you explore these various views, keep in mind that Flew was not looking to find whether or not religious utterances were meaningful but was exploring their scientific status.

1 Explain what kind of scholar Karl Raimund Popper was.

....

....

2 How did Otto Neurath describe Karl Popper?

....

3 In your own words explain Popper's problem with the logical positivists.

....

....

....

....

....

4 Popper argues that the method of science is not of verification but of falsification. What did he mean by this?

....

....

....

....

....

....

5 What was the *University* debate?

....

....

6 Who was Anthony Flew?

....

....

....

7 In your own words write out the key ideas in Wisdom's parable of the gardener.

....

....

....

....

....

....

....

8 What conclusions does Flew draw from this parable?

....

....

9 Explain what Flew means by 'the death of a thousand qualifications'.

....

....

10 Explain, in your own words, what R. M. Hare means by a 'blik'.

....

....

....

....

....

11 Explain the distinction between sane and insane bliks.

....

....

....

....

....

12 How does Hick point out vulnerabilities in Hare's position?

....

....

....

....

....

13 Explain Basil Mitchell's response to Flew's challenge during the symposium.

....

....

....

....

....

....

14 Explain how Mitchell believed his parable differs from Hare's lunatic student.

....

....

....

....

15 Explain which of these views, if any, you find most convincing and why.

....

....

....

....

....

....

....

Exam-style question

Plan your answer here then write the answer itself on a separate sheet of paper. Allow 40 minutes to write this essay. Use 2 minutes to plan and 2 minutes to reread your essay and correct mistakes.

'The falsification principle offers no real challenge to religious belief.'
Discuss.

`35 marks` `45`

© OCR 2009–13

Topic 7
Wittgenstein and language games

Wittgenstein's *Tractatus*

While it is debatable whether or not Wittgenstein wrote specifically about religious language, his concept of language games has been well used by neo-Wittgensteinians who were interested in the meaningfulness or otherwise of religious utterances. In the *Tractatus Logico-Philosophicus*, Wittgenstein proposed that many of the traditional problems of philosophy were actually problems of language. Along with this he proposed a picture theory of language, suggesting that language could be seen as giving us a pictorial representation of the world. However, he also pointed to the fact that we can rearrange these picture elements so that they no longer directly represent the reality of the world.

Language games

As his philosophical thinking developed, Wittgenstein moved away from both the *Tractatus* and the Vienna Circle. In becoming what scholars refer to as the later Wittgenstein he gave up the belief that we could construct one master logical language. The book we know as *Philosophical Investigations* was published posthumously by his fellow philosophers and pupils. It is said that it was while passing a football match he came up with the idea of language games. The rules from different games make the same actions become either a good move or a foul. A rugby player picking up a ball and running with it is doing what he should; a football player doing the same thing is committing a foul. If we apply this thought to language we can no longer speak of a word having an absolute meaning, we must instead ask how it is being used in a particular context.

In applying this idea to religious statements you need to keep in mind that Wittgenstein believed there were only games and we could not therefore look for the *real* meaning of words. To put it another way, you might say 'God is love', 'God is omnipotent' or 'God is omniscient' within a particular theological language game but you cannot conclude from this that those who are playing the game are talking about a being who exists in the real or objective world. If you hold this to be true then theists and atheists are not only making meaningful statements within their own games but they cannot in reality speak meaningfully to each other, unless they play a different game with shared meaning.

Developments of this view

Among the significant developments of this view were those put forward by D. Z. Phillips. He makes use of the following Wittgensteinian quotation:

> Philosophy may in no way interfere with the actual use of language; it can in the end only describe it. For it cannot give it any foundation either. It leaves everything as it is.

This led Phillips to the belief that the philosopher's task was not to comment on the truth of religious statements, but to question and clarify their meaning. So he is taking a step back and not exploring whether or not it is possible to settle the question of our talking about God but rather to ask what it means to affirm or deny that a man is talking about God. By this he is postulating that it is not the job of philosophers to determine whether God exists or not. As you can see, this philosophical approach opens a can of worms about what we can legitimately expect language to do and it has several significant implications.

1 Write a brief account of Wittgenstein's life.

....

....

....

....

....

....

2 Give an account of the most significant points in the *Tractatus Logico-Philosophicus*.

....

....

....

....

....

....

....

3 Fill in the blank in the following statement. In this book Wittgenstein is most famous for saying:

'Whereof one cannot speak, ...,'

4 Describe in your own words what Wittgenstein meant by language games.

....

....

....

....

....

....

....

5 Explain the problem raised by a believer and a non-believer playing different language games.

....

....

....

....

....

6 Explain the logical problem of the excluded middle.

....

....

....

....

....

7 Explain how Don Cupitt, following an interpretation of Wittgenstein, developed his own views on values and meanings.

....
....
....
....
....
....

8 What is meant by 'forms of life' among neo-Wittgensteinians?

....
....
....
....
....
....
....
....
....
....

9 Explain why D. Z. Phillips believed that it was not the philosopher's job to determine God's existence.

....
....
....
....

10 Outline Patrick Sherry's views on forms of life and religious language.

....
....
....
....
....
....

11 Explain why circularity is a problem for language game theory.

....
....
....
....

⑫ **What are 'performatory utterances'?**

....

....

....

⑬ **Explain what J. L. Austin means by 'locutions'.**

....

....

....

....

....

....

Exam-style question

Plan your answer here then write the answer itself on a separate sheet of paper. Allow 40 minutes to write this essay. Use 2 minutes to plan and 2 minutes to reread your essay and correct mistakes.

Critically assess Wittgenstein's belief that language games allow religious statements to have meaning.

35 marks   45

© OCR 2009–13

....

....

....

....

....

....

....

....

....

....

....

....

....

Topic 8
Revelation and Scripture

Approaching Scripture

A number of philosophical concepts come together in this topic as we look at the God who reveals himself through Holy Scripture. The word 'holy' itself indicates that we are studying, in the eyes of many, more than just random speculations. As well as what we might mean by 'holy', this topic also questions what sort of God we believe in. If, for example, we believe in a God who is outside time rather than the kind of intimate interactive God of the Bible and the Koran we would have a very different view on the significance of scriptures.

It is also important to keep in mind when we approach any kind of scriptures that they not only incorporate the agenda of the writer but also make use of different kinds of writing which therefore carry different kinds of authority within any religion. For example, Scripture can be read in a literal sense, an allegorical sense, a mythical sense, a tropological sense or an anagogical sense.

Along with the issue of different literary styles, since the archaeological discoveries of the nineteenth century onwards, scholars have proposed a wide range of different styles of criticism from the well-known form and redaction criticism to a widening approach to criticising Scripture. In this topic you can also explore a holistic approach through integrating Bultmann's approach to myth with your understanding of the complexities of scriptural interpretation.

Propositional and non-propositional views

Philosophers also explore the traditions of propositional and non-propositional views on both Scripture and faith. The propositional tradition holds that a series of truths, in the form of propositions, make up the content of faith. Individual faith is then an assent to that series of propositions held to be truths. What counts as truths clearly change between different faiths and are not therefore capable of being held as objective truths.

This tradition is often further divided into natural and revealed theology. The first deals with those truths which are knowable through an unaided human intellect — such as a God created this universe. The second needs special revelation such as the belief some denominations have about the Trinity or the Incarnation. This distinction is generally dismissed by those who hold a non-propositional view of revelation.

One way of contrasting non-propositional with propositional is to think of the latter being 'belief in...' rather than 'belief that' a particular group of propositions is true. Non-propositional could be expressed like the psalmist who looking at the beauty of creation writes 'Be still and know that I am God'. Revelation, in this sense, is not a passive thing but would seem to demand a response, a response which human beings are free to make or not.

It is worth keeping in mind as you explore this area of the specification that things are not black and white. There is no easy way to separate the entanglement between these understandings of revelation as, for some, God both reveals himself and utters sentences to be believed. Faith is clearly a much bigger reality for believers than the distinction between propositional and non-propositional revelation.

1 Explain what scholars mean when they say that a full scriptural exegesis involves the following four fold technique:

a the literal sense

b the allegorical sense

c the tropological sense

d the anagogical sense

2 Explain why Erasmus of Rotterdam thought that, in his time, Scripture was in danger of losing its true meaning.

3 Outline the various changes during the Reformation which affected the study of the Bible.

4 In scriptural studies explain what is meant by:

a historical criticism

b form criticism

c textual criticism

d literary criticism

5 How did the twentieth-century fundamentalist movement influence biblical criticism?

6 In your own words what is propositional revelation?

7 In your own words what is non-propositional revelation?

8 Explain the strengths and weaknesses of propositional revelation.

9 Explain the strengths and weaknesses of non-propositional revelation.

10 To what extent is it foolish to believe God communicates with us?

Topic 9
The divine attributes

Attributes of the Christian God

In this topic we will explore the attributes we attach to the Christian God, often expressed as the God of classical theism. Christians believe that God is eternal, omnipotent, omniscient and omnibenevolent.

Issues of eternity and omniscience are at the core of the discussion. In the next topic we will explore the consequences of believing in an omnipotent and benevolent God.

Omnipotence

One of the most common descriptions of the Christian God is that he is omnipotent or all-powerful. As you will remember from your AS course, it is one of the attributes challenged by the Epicurean Triad in discussions about the existence of evil. Some, such as Descartes, have argued that at the extreme God could do anything; though taking the same view as Aquinas most would stop at saying God can do anything which is not logically impossible. Questions such as can God make a square circle were therefore meaningless to Aquinas — an empty concept for which there is no corresponding reality.

To understand what religious believers are trying to say it is better to approach their understanding from the

idea that God is the creative and sustaining power of the universe. However, they also accept that God is limited by the type of universe he chose to create. Christian believers see creation as God bringing about an environment where human beings are able to develop a loving relationship with their God. To do this, Christians use the term 'Almighty' rather than omnipotent.

This resolves philosophical discussion about whether or not God can make a stone so heavy he cannot lift it and allows for a more positivist discussion about this particular attribute. This approach will never challenge the criticisms of scholars such as Richard Dawkins but you could say it has allowed serious debate within this religious language game.

Omnibenevolence

Omnibenevolence, on the other hand, conflates two other concepts about God: the ideas that God is both perfect and morally good. In fact, as you will have seen in your AS studies, for the Jewish faith, God is the source of all moral goodness. What you need to explore is the content of this goodness as this is where much of the dispute lies.

The theological background of any believer seems to bring about different understanding of goodness. Some would say it is found in the justice of God, others in his love and still others in his mercy. None of these concepts is empirically verifiable and all are about faith rather than fact there is no reason to prefer one over the other.

Another philosophical approach which can cast some light on the debate is to look back to Anselm and Descartes and ask what they meant when they said God is perfect. Clearly, at the very least we would look to what a human would expect goodness to be and take it on to a concept of goodness beyond those possible to mere humans.

You should be able to research and write accounts of the many complex questions and attempts to grasp the nature of a God who, if he exists, keeps himself at an epistemic distance from his people. This is also an area where you should be able to demonstrate in an examination your understanding of the holistic nature of so much of this course.

1 In your own words explain what is meant by the omnipotence of God.

....

....

....

....

2 Write out three biblical references which show the Jewish and Christian belief in God's omniscience.

....

....

....

....

....

....

....

3 Complete this quotation from *The God Delusion* by Richard Dawkins:

'it has not escaped the notice of logicians that omniscience and omnipotence are

mutually incompatible. If God is omniscient, he must already ....

....

....,'

4 How would philosophers, such as Thomas Aquinas, reply to this challenge?

....

....

....

....

....

5 In your own words explain what is meant by omnibenevolence.

....

....

....

6 What do philosophers mean when they say that God is perfect?

....

....

....

....

7 Write out three quotations from the Bible which attest to the Jewish and Christian belief in an omnibenevolent God.

....

....

....

....

....

8 Given the alleged epistemic distance between God and his people, is there any point in discussing whether or not God is omnipotent and omnibenevolent?

....

....

....

....

....

....

Exam-style question

Plan your answer here then write the answer itself on a separate sheet of paper. Allow 40 minutes to write this essay. Use 2 minutes to plan and 2 minutes to reread your essay and correct mistakes.

Evaluate the philosophical problems raised by believing that God is eternal.

35 marks 45

© OCR 2009–13

....

....

....

....

....

....

....

....

....

....

....

Topic 10
Boethius on divine foreknowledge

Boethius' understanding of eternity

Crucial to understanding Boethius' position is his understanding of eternity. If you do not understand that, you will not understand what he meant by divine foreknowledge having a questionable status. He was specifically looking at how God can be all loving and at the same time know of future evil in the world.

In his book *The Consolation of Philosophy* Boethius writes as if he is having a conversation with a fictional Lady Philosophy. His *theodicy* is strikingly different from those of Augustine and Irenaeus in that he, despite being a Christian, would seem to have described a God who is more deist than theist. By this I mean that he proposes a God outside time who sees the whole history of the universe, past and future, in one moment. This is what he calls 'the simultaneous possession of boundless life made clearer by comparison with temporal things'.

One of the methods I find useful to get my head around this concept when teaching Boethius is always to talk about God's knowledge in the present tense. So do not think about what God may foresee you doing but only what God *sees* you doing. In this way Boethius is able to argue that God cannot influence our actions since he does not know *in advance* what any of us is going to do.

Lady Philosophy, however, challenges Boethius with the thought that if God knows about our actions in any sense then those actions are necessary actions. She asks:

> 'Why then, do you think that the things which Providence sees in its eternal present are governed by necessity whereas the things which you see in your present you do not regard as being governed by necessity'.

Simple and conditional necessity

This led Boethius to propose that there are two kinds of necessity: simple or absolute necessity and conditional necessity. He uses the story of a man sitting on a hill watching the sun shining and a man walking. The simple necessity is seen in the shining of the sun which is part of the way the universe works and is a necessity of nature. However, the man chooses to walk and Boethius describes this as a conditional necessity.

It is important in looking at conditional necessity to focus on the nature of the act. Whatever we choose to do God does not influence the nature of the act. The man has voluntarily chosen to walk for his own reason and it is clear that God has not influenced this decision in any way. This allows Boethius to argue that God's providence, a word he uses instead of prevision, has

no effect on the man and leaves God's ability to judge in place. This is where he is taking the argument — he wants to say that when God rewards and punishes his people he does so justly. This is because from his eternal present he sees but does not affect actions which from our perspective are both future and free.

There are many criticisms of this position, but one of the most effective is to question the extent to which Boethius is faithful to a belief in the God of classical theism. As I said above, we seem to be discussing a more deist God than a theist God. So, for example, how would Boethius explain the Christian belief in the incarnation if he is arguing for a God who is outside time and who does not interact with humanity?

1 Write a brief account of the life of Boethius.

....

....

....

....

....

....

2 Summarise the five aims and methods of Book 5, Chapter 6 of *The Consolation of Philosophy*.

....

....

....

....

....

....

3 Explain what Boethius means when he says that what is known depends on the nature of the knower.

....

....

....

....

....

....

....

4 Explain the significance for Boethius of God being eternal.

....

....

....

....

....

5 Complete the following quotation from *The Consolation of Philosophy*:

'Eternity is the simultaneous possession of boundless life which is made clearer by

comparison with temporal things. This becomes clear when we ....

....

....

....

and no longer exists in yesterday.'

6 Explain the difference, for Boethius, of providence and prevision.

....

....

....

....

....

7 Explain in your own words the distinction Boethius makes between two kinds of necessity.

....

....

....

....

....

....

....

8 Instead of the man on the hill, make up your own example to describe the difference between simple and conditional necessity.

....

....

....

....

....

....

....

9 Complete the following quotation:

'The difference between simple and conditional necessity is ....

.... ,

10 When discussing free actions what does Boethius mean when he says we need to examine the nature of the act?

....

....

....

....

....

11 Is Boethius right to say that God distributes rewards and punishments justly?

....

....

....

....

....

....

12 To what extent is the notion of a timeless God coherent?

....

....

....

....

....

....

13 Is it possible to reconcile the distant watching God of Boethius with the God of the Bible?

....

....

....

....

....

....

14 To what extent might modern science support a Boethian view of time and eternity?

....

....

....

....

....

....

Exam-style question

Plan your answer here then write the answer itself on a separate sheet of paper. Allow 40 minutes to write this essay. Use 2 minutes to plan and 2 minutes to reread your essay and correct mistakes.

To what extent was Boethius successful in his argument that God rewards and punishes justly?

`35 marks` `45`

© OCR 2009–13

....

....

....

....

....

....

Topic 11
Body and soul identity

Do human beings have a soul?

The question of whether or not human beings have a soul has preoccupied humankind for as long as we have existed. At one end of the debate are the reductionists who would maintain that we are organic machines and at the other is the Cartesian view that our soul lives within our body and will survive our death. In a rough way, these can be described as monist and dualist views. Along with these are more complex understandings of body-soul relationships. Terms which you will need to be able to explain include: dualism, substance dualism, monism and materialism.

Plato, Aristotle and Aquinas

One of the earliest debates in this area was between Plato and his pupil Aristotle. Plato saw the soul as something which pre-existed the body and would pass back to the world of the Forms after death. Aristotle, on the other hand, in most of his writings, saw the soul as making the body work but ceasing to exist at the same time as a body ceases to function. Christianity adds another layer to this by believing, as expressed in the Apostle's Creed, in bodily resurrection.

Thomas Aquinas, following the Aristotelian tradition, rejects Plato's idea that sensation was simply a function of the soul and that a soul made use of a body and argues: 'it is clear that man is not a soul only but something composed of soul and body'.

As you will see in the next topic, this belief, since we know our bodies will not survive death, has led to many philosophical attempts to reconcile the idea of surviving death with a body, whether it is the replica suggested by Hick's thought experiment or the glorified body proposed by Aquinas.

Descartes, Ryle and Dawkins

Descartes holds a completely different position. He proposes that the body and soul are separate substances. This led him to suggest that possibly the pineal gland is the link between these two substances. When you explore this area you will find not only issues of a poor understanding of human physiology but serious issues of how the soul can affect the body. Those looking for some 'stretch and challenge' may, in this context, wish to look at the work of Roger Penrose on the question of consciousness taking place at the quantum level.

In looking at Descartes' position, Gilbert Ryle accuses him of committing a category error. By this he means that Descartes incorrectly assumed that mind and matter are of the same logical type. Ryle maintained that they are not, even if descriptions of mind and matter look superficially similar.

Finally you will also need to explore the views of Richard Dawkins and what he means by 'soul one' and 'soul two'. This is probably the best example of a hard materialist position leading us back in a sense to the Aristotelian view that the body and soul are one, though the soul is not the form of the body as it was for Aristotle.

1 Briefly explain the meaning of the following terms:

dualism ....

substance dualism ....

monism ....

materialism ....

2 Explain why Plato believed that while the body is temporary and corruptible the soul lives on.

....

....

....

....

3 Explain Aristotle's understanding of the soul.

....

....

....

....

4 Explain one of the early Christian heresies which made the Church define its understanding of the body/soul identity.

....

....

....

....

....

5 How did Thomas Aquinas develop philosophical understanding of the soul?

....

....

....

....

....

6 Explain what Descartes was doing when he concluded *'Cogito ergo sum'*.

....

....

....

....

7 Explain the Cartesian view on the existence of a soul.

....

....

....

....

8 Ryle thought Descartes had made a category error. Outline one of his examples to demonstrate this theory.

....

....

....

....

9 Explain why these beliefs do not mean that Ryle is a materialist.

....

....

....

....

....

10 To what extent are Dawkins' views on soul one and soul two coherent?

....

....

....

....

....

11 Explain John Hick's view on the soul.

....

....

....

....

....

Exam-style question

Answer the following question on a separate sheet of paper. Allow 40 minutes to write this essay. Use 2 minutes to plan and 2 minutes to reread your essay and correct mistakes.

Evaluate the claim that the body is distinct from the soul.   35 marks

Topic 12
Beliefs about life after death

Bodily resurrection

There are a number of topics which are important to grasp for this part of the course: resurrection, reincarnation, disembodied existence and embodied existence after death. Make sure you check what different groups actually believe and do not just assume that the common understanding is right. Many Christians, for example, speak as if they are dualist, talking of the body dying and the soul rising to eternal life. In fact the Apostles' Creed is very clear about bodily resurrection. However it is less clear about what a risen body might be like or indeed, outside Scripture, whether there is any reason for us to believe in life after death.

Aquinas tried to resolve the monist/dualist issue by proposing that there may be a time after death when the soul is somewhere lacking its fullness and waiting to be united with a glorified body. From this Aquinas suggested a beatific vision as the ultimate goal of human existence. In this way he tried to unite Aristotelian and early medieval philosophy.

John Hick attempted a thought experiment to try to suggest a way bodily survival post death might be possible. His thought experiment proposes a replica being created in another place after death. He is trying to explain how it might be possible to believe in a God who could recreate or reconstitute a human psycho-physical individual. It is important to remember that Hick did not believe that this *thought experiment* succeeded.

Disembodied existence and reincarnation

One of the places to look to explore the issue of disembodied existence is the work of H. H. Price. He suggested a world where disembodied 'souls' exist as some sort of dream images. These 'souls' might communicate with similar souls through some sort of telepathy and he suggests they might retain some sort of image of their bodies.

A possible scientific route to assessing this area would be to look at the case of a woman called Pam Reynolds. To remove an embolism from her brain stem, doctors turned off all electrical activity in her brain and yet she was able to describe the tools they used during the operation and the music playing in the theatre. This and other 'paranormal' activities may or may not be counted as support for a philosophical position which holds that some sort of spiritual survival after death is possible. You will need to assess the material for yourself and, whichever position attracts you, remember in examinations to support your view with argument and not just to state a belief.

Hindu teachings on reincarnation can also be an interesting area for study as another form of dualism. As you will see as you explore these views, part of the problem is that there is little evidence of memories of past lives and therefore there are questions about personal identity and continuity.

Reasons for believing in an afterlife

Finally, this area of the specification asks you to consider another holistic issue — namely the question of whether or not we need to believe in some sort of afterlife in order to resolve many of the issues raised by the existence of evil and suffering. Atheists, such as Richard Dawkins, might agree with George Orwell in *Animal Farm* and say that religion promises a Sugar Candy Mountain, but a theist position may be that much of the evil humanity suffers can be justified only if God has a higher plan for us all.

1 In your own words write brief definitions of the following terms:

resurrection ....

....

reincarnation ....

....

disembodied existence ....

....

embodied existence post death ....

....

2 Explain what the Fourth Lateran Council taught about resurrection.

....

....

....

....

....

....

3 The promise of an end to death is found in Scripture. Write out the following:

Isaiah 25:8 ....

....

1 Corinthians 15:26 ....

....

4 Outline the four qualities St Paul believed a risen body would have.

....

....

....

....

....

....

5 What did Thomas Aquinas mean by the beatific vision?

....

....

....

....

....

6 Outline and explain Hick's replica theory.

....

....

....

....

....

....

....

7 Explain how H. H. Price or a similar philosopher proposed post-death disembodied existence might be possible.

....

....

....

....

....

....

8 Explain Hindu beliefs about reincarnation and karma.

....

....

....

....

....

....

9 Explain Peter Geach's critique of the concept of reincarnation.

....

....

....

....

....

10 To what extent can the existence of evil be justified by the existence of heaven and hell?

....

....

....

....

....

....

....

11 'Belief in any form of life after death is incoherent.' Discuss.

Exam-style question

Plan your answer here then write the answer itself on a separate sheet of paper. Allow 40 minutes to write this essay. Use 2 minutes to plan and 2 minutes to reread your essay and correct mistakes.

'Resurrection is more likely than reincarnation.' Discuss.

35 marks **45**

© OCR 2009–13

Philip Allan, an imprint of Hodder Education, an Hachette UK company, Market Place, Deddington, Oxfordshire, OX15 0SE

Orders
Bookpoint Ltd, 130 Milton Park, Abingdon, Oxfordshire OX14 4SB
tel: 01235 827827
fax: 01235 400401
e-mail: education@bookpoint.co.uk
Lines are open 9.00 a.m.–5.00 p.m., Monday to Saturday, with a 24-hour message answering service. You can also order through **www.hoddereducation.co.uk**

© Hugh Campbell 2014
ISBN 978-1-4718-0009-2
First printed 2014
Impression number 5 4 3 2 1
Year 2019 2018 2017 2016 2015 2014

Printed in Dubai

Hachette UK's policy is to use papers that are natural, renewable and recyclable products and made from wood grown in sustainable forests. The logging and manufacturing processes are expected to conform to the environmental regulations of the country of origin.

P02295

PHILIP ALLAN FOR
HODDER
EDUCATION

ISBN 978-1-4718-0009-2

9 781471 800092